NYC Scavenger

R. C. Staab

Library of Congress Control Number: 2022949324

ISBN: 9781681064338

Cover and interior design by Claire Ford

Cover and interior photos by the author. Author photo by Victor Macaluso.

Printed in the United States of America
23 24 25 26 27 5 4 3 2 1

Dedication

To my parents, Joan Badzgon and Bob Staab,
for trusting me and giving me the latitude to explore,

To Kathy Hug for her thoughtful critique,
never-ending enthusiasm, and encouragement for my writing,

And to my wife, Valari, who, despite thinking I'm crazy
to take on another project, always supports and loves me.

Contents

Introduction

Ask New Yorkers about the significance of Manhattan, and they will certainly agree that the borough is the Center of the Universe.

With apologies to the other four boroughs—Brooklyn, Queens, the Bronx, and Staten Island—the island of Manhattan is what people envision when they think of New York City. In the United States, Manhattan has the tallest buildings, the wealthiest financial institutions, the most exciting Broadway shows, and the greatest art museums, plus 1.6 million residents jammed into an island that's barely longer than 13 miles and is only about two miles at its widest.

So, by necessity, creating a Manhattan scavenger hunt is about choosing from thousands of possibilities.

Whether you are a first-time visitor looking for an ingenious way to explore the city or a resident with an interest in exploring beyond your neighborhood, this book offers a different way to explore this wondrous metropolis. As you search for the answers to the riddles, you're likely to discover whimsical places, historic sites, and hidden streets that even the most jaded Manhattanites might never have seen.

How to Create Your Own Scavenger Hunt

By design, *New York City Scavenger* is focused on geography—15 sections heading north from Downtown Manhattan, zig-zagging back and forth from the East River to the Hudson River, until they reach the northernmost neighborhood of Inwood.

Other than the gerrymandered area of the Lower Hudson River that includes Battery Park City and the Meatpacking District, most of the sections are clearly defined. Some sections include adjacent neighborhoods, particularly in the tangled web of Manhattan south of 14th Street. Unlike most other American cities, all these sites are easily reachable via the subway, bus, and on foot, with the suggestion you wear hiking boots in the hilly section of Inwood.

Each neighborhood or section features at least 23 clues to unlock. Each clue includes a four-line riddle, an illustration, and a photograph typically of a close-up of part of some of the nation's tallest skyscrapers, world-class museums, mouth-watering restaurants, famous statues, unusual streets and homes, and decorative subway stations.

How to start? My suggestion is that you sit down with friends, family, or classmates and dig into the riddles with the help of a computing device or a map. Come up with potential answers. Armed with the book or your notes, start exploring your neighborhood of choice to match each image in the book with the site. These days, everyone's phone is a camera, so you can easily share your answers with your friends or competitors.

All clues include a photographic image—99 percent of which can be viewed 24/7 from the street, sidewalk, or inside a public park. The few photos taken indoors are from places that never sleep (that's a clue right there!).

Finding the clues gives you an opportunity to examine the unusual history of out-of-the-way sites or learn more about the iconic places for which New York City is famous. If you really get stuck, email us at nycscavenger@gmail.com for hints.

If a geographic scavenger hunt doesn't suit you, there are more than 350 clues in the book that can be reassembled to create unique scavenger hunts, such as:

- Pop culture: famous sites where movies or TV shows were filmed
- Animals and marine life: dogs, cats, fish, and even a wolf
- Broadway theaters and performance halls
- Restaurants across a variety of ethnic and food types
- Art and art museums
- Shopping sites large and small

Detailed special interest tours are annotated on our website at www.nycscavenger.com.

New York City Scavenger is your chance to experience every inch of the island of Manhattan. So, get out there and explore. And then brag about it, like any good New Yorker would do.

Legend

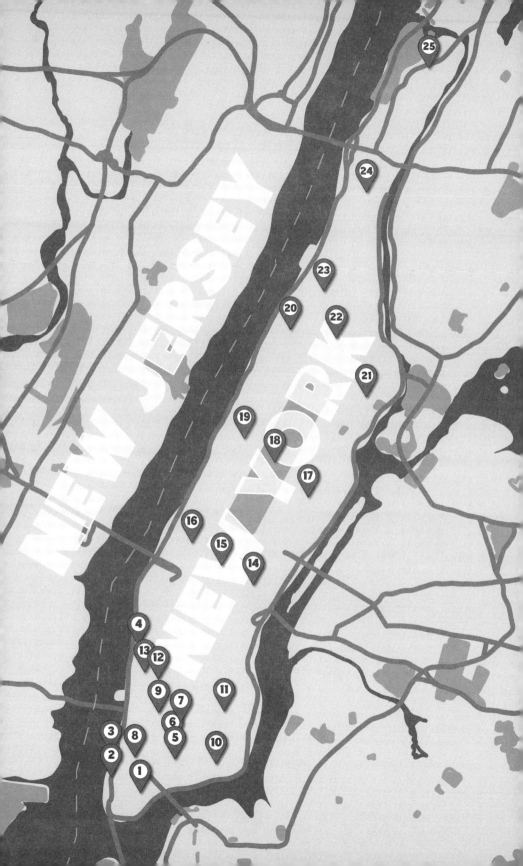

Downtown: Battery Park, Financial Center, & Civic Center

The King in *Alice's Adventures in Wonderland* declares, "Begin at the beginning and go on till you come to the end. . . ." There is no better place to head down the rabbit hole for a scavenger hunt of the island of Manhattan than Downtown—New York Harbor to the south, the East River to the East, plus sites and surprises east of West Street and south of Canal Street and the Brooklyn Bridge.

1

The face above the eastern door
May help you know what is "in store."
There's one in Washington, DC,
All visitors see both for free.

2

An alien who flew to earth
And landed on this shipping berth
Could get a ride without a fee
From Yankee Park to Battery.

3

She's reproduced in foreign lands.
She moved one time from where she stands.
She advocates diverse worksites.
She's raising up her gender's rights.

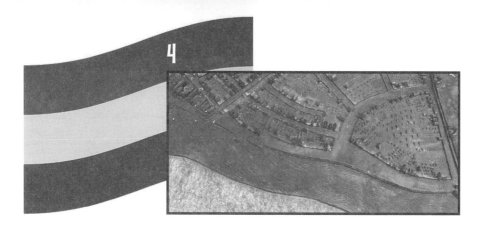

Upon this rock you'll find a plaque,
That shows the oldest plan around.
Before they flew the Union Jack
They settled here and plowed the ground.

_____

_____

From Brooklyn Heights, you see this park.
It's high above the water mark.
You escalate from grey to green,
One-acre square where gardeners preen.

_____

_____

6

In all the world, they view his stride.
It takes some guts to join his ride.
The tail is down, but he looks up.
To him, the winners raise a cup.

7

About as old as Washington,
It's seen the war and wrecking cranes.
You bring a friend to have some fun
Or learn about gallant campaigns.

8

The slanted building looks askew.
The glass and mirrors show it's new.
Amidst the whish of white oak trees,
Descend the stairs for memories.

_____

_____

9

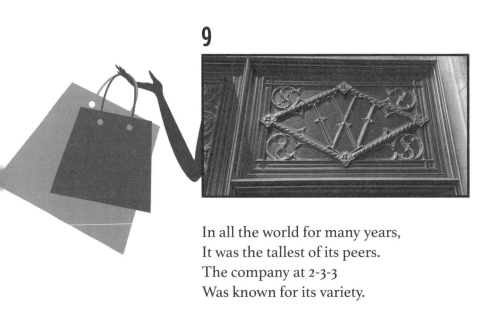

In all the world for many years,
It was the tallest of its peers.
The company at 2-3-3
Was known for its variety.

_____

_____

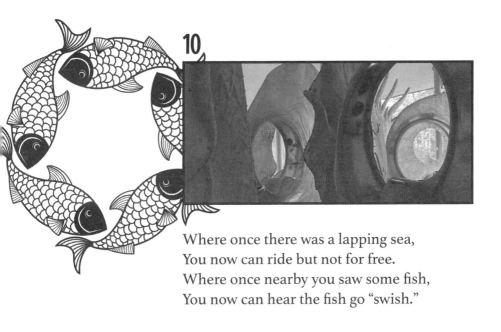

Where once there was a lapping sea,
You now can ride but not for free.
Where once nearby you saw some fish,
You now can hear the fish go "swish."

11

No need to keep apace with him.
He stands nearby the campus gym.
The sale of these raised millions for
Those dogs who rescued many more.

12

An African who has been freed,
A priest, a Jew, and those in need
Comprise this monument to those
Who often came with just their clothes.

13

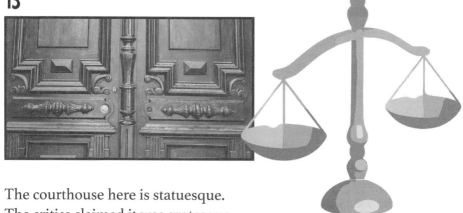

The courthouse here is statuesque.
The critics claimed it was grotesque
And not because of its design.
The "boss" used it as his gold mine.

14

A hurricane blew through this pier.
It nearly closed—that was the fear.
But restaurants are sparkling new.
Atop the roof, you'll find a queue.

15

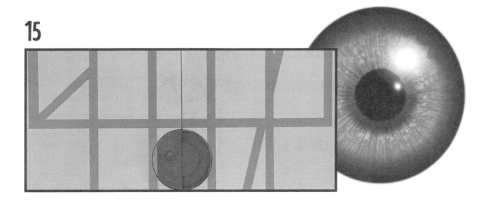

The logo on these humble doors
Will open wide to trains and stores.
The Pantheon has one of these,
But this is taller by degrees.

16

The lady can be seen through this,
But pause to think and reminisce
About a war which many fought,
Though some call it a war forgot.

_____

_____

17

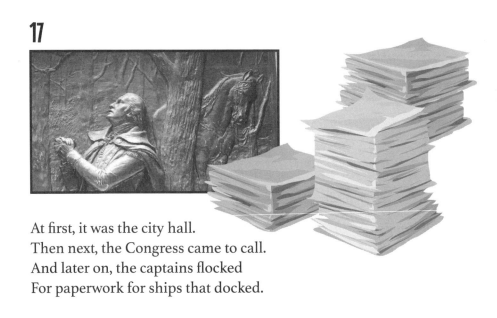

At first, it was the city hall.
Then next, the Congress came to call.
And later on, the captains flocked
For paperwork for ships that docked.

_____

_____

18

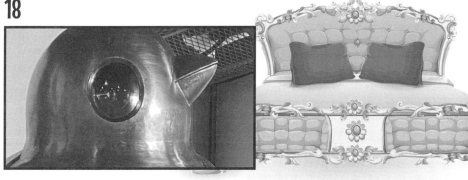

A famous brand came to this place
To rent some rooms and party space.
The Beaux Arts style gives it some flair.
The bird's below the porte cochere.

_____

_____

19

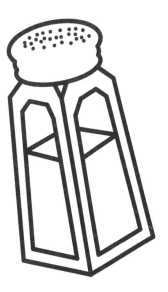

The sign's been there a century,
The salted fish a memory.
An outpost for a rendezvous
Is now a place to have a brew.

_____

_____

20

Behind the gate, beneath the tree,
Is sacred ground that's one of three.
Some souls that rest and always stay,
They come alive on old Broadway.

_____

_____

21

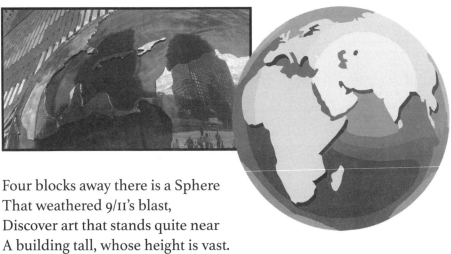

Four blocks away there is a Sphere
That weathered 9/11's blast,
Discover art that stands quite near
A building tall, whose height is vast.

_____

_____

She oversaw a charity.
She blesses men who sail to sea.
She was the first American
When named so by a "fisherman."

23

You "peck" along the riverside,
The bridge in view at every stride.
Then walk one block from taller ships
To see this slip near grassy strips.

Battery Park City, Lower Hudson Park, & Meatpacking District

Battery Park City is a large residential community west of West Street. Our scavenger hunt begins north of Battery Park City—staying west of West Street—along the Hudson River to 14th Street and includes the invigorated Meatpacking District west of Hudson Street and north of Houston Street.

1

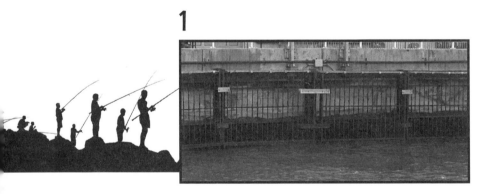

The fishermen enjoy the pier,
But that's not why the building's here.
A tunnel far beneath these shores
Needs this shaft from which air pours.

2

A leading force in all that's wired,
Its screen inside is never tired.
You see the show as you go by.
This flagship store will catch your eye.

_____

_____

3

It's landscaped as a no-man's land.
Beyond the plants, the rocks, and sand,
You find this place for players small
With a slide, 33 feet tall.

_____

_____

4

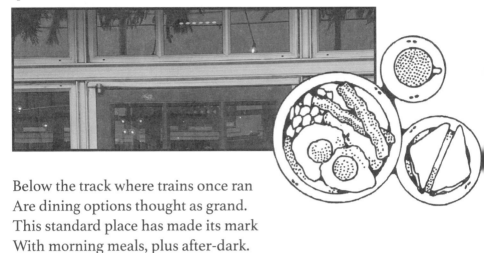

Below the track where trains once ran
Are dining options thought as grand.
This standard place has made its mark
With morning meals, plus after-dark.

_____

_____

5

The Whitney space includes his art.
To see these two you have to start
Along the esplanade with views,
Where you can take a harbor cruise.

_____

_____

6

The "Twister" by the riverside,
It may seem like a coaster ride,
But what the artist holds as key
Are forms experienced at sea.

7

John Jacob Astor bought the land
To build an edifice that's grand.
Before there was *New York* or *US*,
The tenant's news created fuss.

8

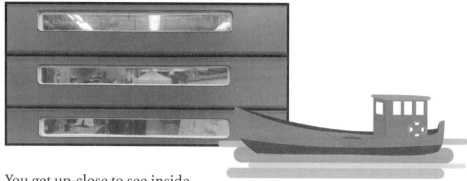

You get up-close to see inside
The place that keeps the "crafts" bone-dry.
When May returns, sign up to ride.
You must know how to swim to try.

_____

_____

9

Along this pier, the ships embark,
While overhead, the autos park.
And if you're looking for a thrill,
Don't take the flight without the skill.

_____

_____

10

From subway trains, you tunnel through.
With water taxis, you get there, too.
Two giant "trees" with trunks of steel
Will welcome those who seek a meal.

11

It represents a foreign land
With windy cliffs above the sand.
A scarcity of "daily bread"
Became the reason that they fled.

12

Below the ground you find a vault.
At level ground, you raise a malt.
While upstairs, Hollywood has shot
A lovers' tryst that was for naught.

13

*Courtesy Linden Hyatt
via Wikimedia Commons*

A granite bench of somber black
Is more tranquil than any plaque.
To honor those who left our sphere,
You contemplate when you sit here.

14

The wind blows through and turns the art
Above the ground in varied parts.
This park is like the *Twilight Zone*,
But on a scale that is full-blown.

15

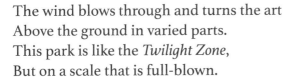

The resilience of these compare
To New Yorkers everywhere.
They filter all the waterways
And hang on piers for many days.

16

A woman gave this place her name.
Her goal: promoting others' fame.
From down to up and then retrace,
It's grown threefold to fill the space.

_____

_____

17

Escape the noise inside the grove
That lies beside this quiet cove,
And climb the ramp above the fray
With Jersey sites across the way.

_____

_____

Above the waves, it has no pier.
Manhattan's only one is here.
Professionals who play this game
Tee up by kids; the game's the same.

19

The appellation's known by all.
It's made of bronze and hardly small.
The man who brought the art to life
Received acclaim, just like his wife.

20

From Patti Smith to Taj Mahal,
From sipping reds to alcohol,
The city pairs the drinks with acts
And offers meals or only snacks.

_____

_____

21

The eco plan's a treasure trove,
A tidal zone, a woodland grove.
You walk among the living things.
Enjoy the sights from both the swings.

_____

_____

22

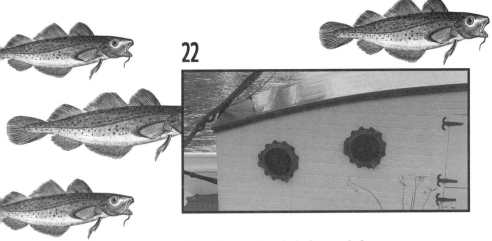

The place they fish for cod the most
Is famously far from the coast.
The boat's new name reflects that "ground"
But stays at dock and serves "a round."

23

Look close: this portal gives a clue.
It is opaque. You can't see through.
You raise a pint and drink some more,
Pretending you are at the shore.

Chinatown, Little Italy, & Nolita

Once a person walks north of city hall and the Financial District, the sights and smells of Chinatown and Little Italy await, plus the revitalized and renamed area north of Little Italy called Nolita. This scavenger hunt section is east of Broadway, north of Chambers Street, and west of Forsythe Street, and includes the area between the Manhattan and Brooklyn bridges.

1

It shines for all both day and night,
And time and temp are shown in light.
The name reflects another time
When penny press was in its prime.

2

When shovels dug into this ground,
A sacred place was all around,
Of thousands who helped build this town.
A history was lost, then found.

3

In Chinatown, there are but two.
These "guards" outside will beckon you.
All welcome here to meditate
And ponder long your worldly fate.

4

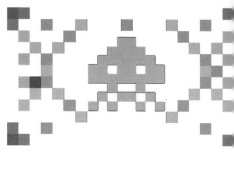

The busy street of Mulberry
Has outdoor stalls like Italy.
The sign above the seafood store
Is one New Yorkers all adore.

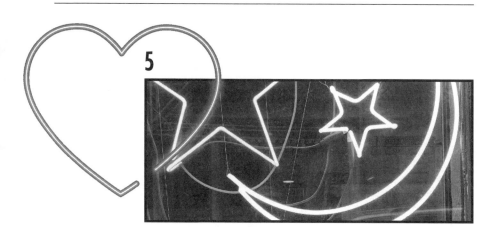

5

The Times Square lights are made of this.
When they are out or go amiss,
They call the team that runs this shop,
And once again the lights will pop.

6

The immigrants we called Chinese
Were settled here from distant seas.
Your journey starts without a fee
To understand why they did flee.

7

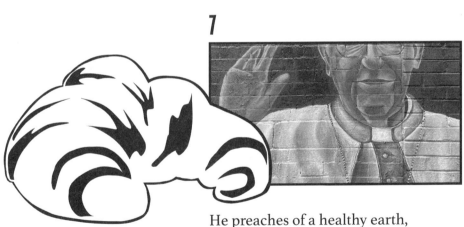

He preaches of a healthy earth,
A blessed life from death to birth.
It's not where you'd expect his face.
A sweetly scent pervades this place.

8

The restoration was first-class,
Including stunning window glass
To recognize the settlers' sweat
While paying forward history's debt.

9

The face is known in Hollywood
But not linked to this neighborhood.
It's part of an ambitious start,
A product of nonprofit art.

10

*Courtesy Ira Rusetskaya
via Vecteezy*

It's no surprise this plaza bears
The sayings of a man who shares
A wisdom learned from careful thought,
And not of men who could be bought.

11

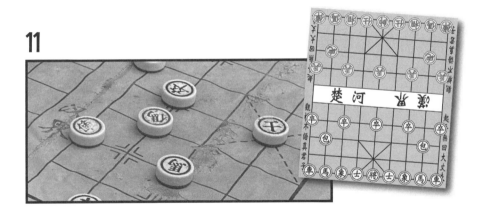

There were five roads that came to meet.
Where gangs once ruled, all feared the street.
But now some meet for other aims
To follow famous Chinese games.

12

The structures near that rise above
Have web addresses with a "gov."
For many years this was a pond,
To which the name does correspond.

13

The faithful here come for the food,
While others like its gangster mood.
And if you hear the word "goombah,"
They're likely fans of cinema.

14

It was a den of opium,
A past that it has overcome.
Sophistication is the rule,
At this stylish nightly jewel.

15

His eminence is known to all,
A "father" to both old and small.
He lived not far from where he "stays,"
Where people stop and give their praise.

16

What is so great about the name?
The diners here bestowed its fame
For Cantonese cuisine first-rate
And for those who do stay up late.

_____

_____

17

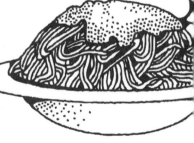

The roots of this "First Family"
Are traced back to old Napoli.
That's where they learned their baking style.
So taste a slice and get a smile.

_____

_____

18

Two hundred feet, a street not long,
Is infamous for what went wrong:
The dens, the homes of ill repute,
And lives of many destitute.

19

A stunning site, the classic dome:
Below it now some call it home.
Before, it was a place to nest,
You didn't want to be a guest.

20

Behind this wall and nearby gate
Are those who many celebrate.
Below the ground, you take a tour
To learn of more and those obscure.

21

On these two blocks of Chinatown,
That's where you let your hair hang down.
The equine flies across the street.
It's made of something you can eat.

22

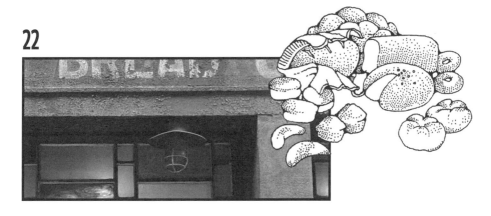

For many years, the lines would form
For bread that rose above the norm.
Before the bakery was here,
It's where you found a fireman's gear.

23

Ten decades in, most people come
For a taste of the first dim sum.
The dumplings have been famed for years.
Just take some home as souvenirs.

Tribeca & SoHo

Two areas formerly known for industry and warehousing have been transformed into some of the hippest neighborhoods in Manhattan—Tribeca (aka the Triangle Below Canal Street) and SoHo (south of Houston Street). To take family and friends on this section of the scavenger hunt, stay south of Houston Street, east of West Street, north of Chambers Street, and west of Lafayette and Broadway.

1

You come to learn or be inspired,
Even though he is long retired.
His legacy goes well beyond
The sport where he first made a bond.

2

Here is where you look for help
Or hear a bark from those who yelp.
Don't call these guys if you see slime,
Because they're working on our dime.

3

The Hudson once lapped very near,
So sailors often stopped for beer.
Two hundred years, it's stayed the same,
A fact that they will gladly claim.

4

This subway view of Union Square
Is down the stairs in open air.
One walks a mile from near that park
To see this view when you embark.

5

There is a "bean" in Illinois
That visitors will oft enjoy.
There is one now nicknamed the same
That's at a place dubbed for a game.

6

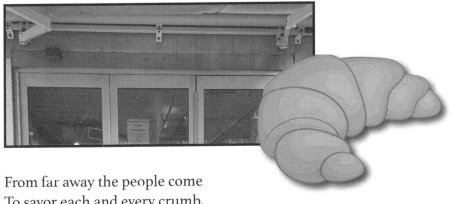

From far away the people come
To savor each and every crumb.
The bakery that made this treat
Combined two "doughs" and made them sweet.

7

No bikes or walking underground,
Yet here's a door, not simply found.
It's right next to the interstate,
The one that ends with number eight.

8

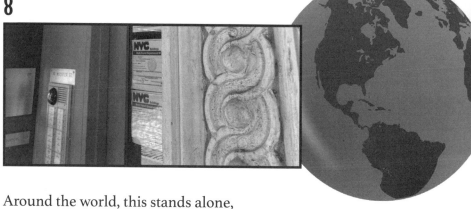

Around the world, this stands alone,
A place with earth where nothing's grown.
A million bucks is its value,
But rarely will one find a queue.

_____

_____

9

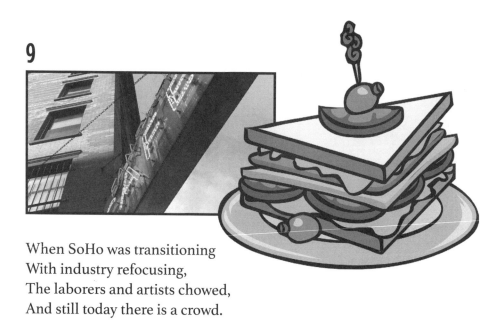

When SoHo was transitioning
With industry refocusing,
The laborers and artists chowed,
And still today there is a crowd.

_____

_____

10

The Avenue is famous for
Latin heroes who cause ardor
This statue of an activist
Is in a square that's often missed.

11

At Station A, there is no train
Or mail that's sent in ice or rain.
The firm inside is widely known.
So head on over with your phone.

12

The sign that's here above the street
Points to a place that's obsolete.
To find this site, go east of West,
Below a place to take a test.

13

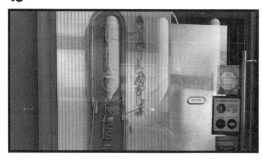

Note two reasons to pay the price.
The first one is for frozen ice.
The second one is for the "shoots"
You post to show your attributes.

14

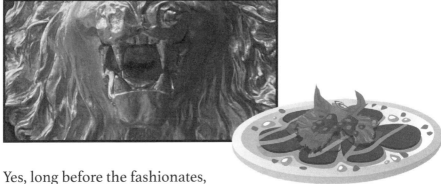

Yes, long before the fashionates,
One came here to drink with your mates.
They're serving still what they call grub,
A SoHo joint that's still a pub.

15

A queer art home and catalyst
Whose artwork may have once been missed,
This museum preserves and saves
And garners praise and often raves.

16

Developers went on a spree
In early 19th century.
These simple homes have gone away.
Historic folk hope these will stay.

17

This cast-iron bridge and alleyway
Connects two sites where people stay.
But years ago, when you were ill,
You sought this place for healing skill.

18

The artist sought no one's input
To make the work that's underfoot.
One walks along this "royal" street
To find this art where two roads meet.

19

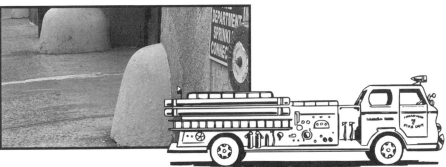

Today they shop and visit here
To see machines and fighting gear,
The bravery of those who stand
And pass a hose from hand to hand.

20

When spring is sprung, the palms appear.
The mezcal bar will offer beer.
Convene inside to meditate,
Experience a lovely date.

21

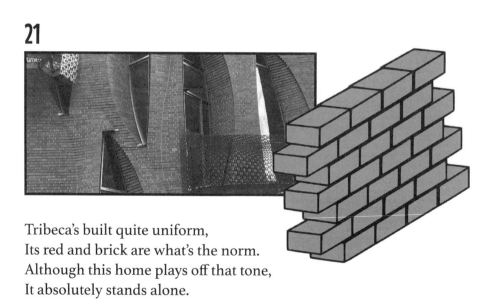

Tribeca's built quite uniform,
Its red and brick are what's the norm.
Although this home plays off that tone,
It absolutely stands alone.

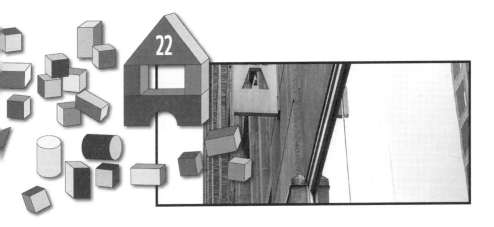

A place that artists celebrate,
Where kids and adults congregate.
A hundred years of art and more,
A world of work one can explore.

23

Its "brutal" style can leave some cold,
Because downtown it breaks the mold.
There's nothing here you can peruse,
Due to a lack of windowed views.

Lower East Side
& East Village

Historically a home for European immigrants newly arrived to Manhattan, the Lower East Side remains a melting pot today. To its north is the equally diverse East Village, which features nightlife and trendy places to eat. The East River is the major eastern border of this scavenger hunt. This area includes Stuyvesant Town and the area south of 14th Street, with the Bowery and Fourth Avenue forming its western border.

1

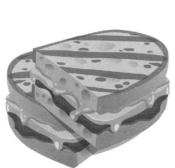 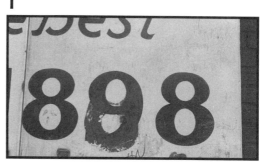

There used to be hundreds of these:
"I'll take the pastrami, please."
Iceland was once part of its name
Before it found its rightful fame.

2

Lady Gaga and Norah Jones
Plus famous bands and some unknowns
Have played inside this tiny hall.
The calendar boasts acts for all.

3

A TV show helped renovate
This tiny space that's long and straight.
To see where fruit and veggies grow,
One ventures down most any row.

4

To showcase artists of today,
Rather than those long passed away,
This sleekly modern place stands out
Along a major north-south route.

_____

_____

5

This place will take one back in time,
Immigration was at its prime.
With interesting simple props,
See apartments and trademen's shops.

_____

_____

6

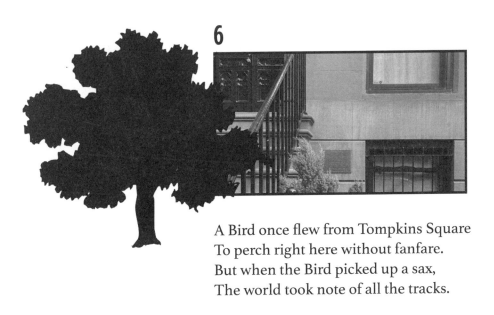

A Bird once flew from Tompkins Square
To perch right here without fanfare.
But when the Bird picked up a sax,
The world took note of all the tracks.

7

For Puerto Rican/Latinx,
This is a center that's complex.
It started as a public school.
Today it is an artist's jewel.

8

Don't tap upon the windowpane.
Do come inside to ease the strain
Of daily life and the rat race:
A "purrfect" store for face-to-face.

9

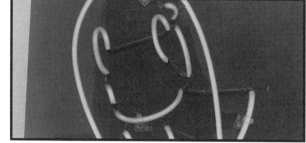

The only one on Essex Street,
Though there once was almost a fleet
Of stores that sold this staple treat.
Now tourists come around to eat.

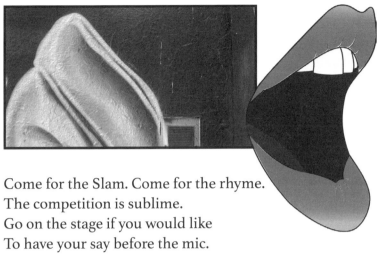

Come for the Slam. Come for the rhyme.
The competition is sublime.
Go on the stage if you would like
To have your say before the mic.

11

A treat from New Orleans is sold
Along with sweets for young and old.
This crazy place has lots of signs
And often people queued in lines.

12

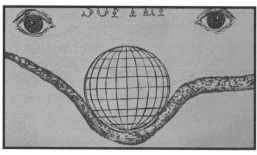

Broadway comes here to have a view,
To see something that's often new:
Experimental plays and shows.
Nearby are "workshops" by the pros.

13

When people hear the place's name,
They know it has a greater aim
Than making soup to serve each day.
They help so many find their way.

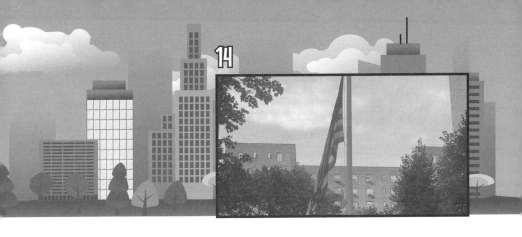

14

Where gas was stored in storage tanks,
This "town" was formed on riverbanks.
It broke the grid of nearby blocks,
With grassy parks to take long walks.

15

Eliza Hamilton lived here.
So did Trotsky, a different year.
From grunge to punks, to K-Pop's craze,
This block evolves from phase to phase.

16

The power of a single frame
Has brought attention and acclaim.
From all the world they will descend
To see, to read, to comprehend.

17

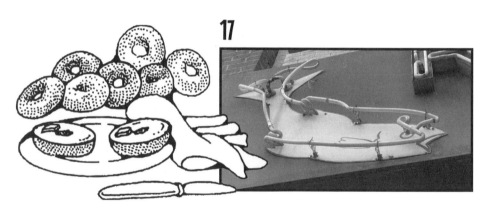

An "appetizer" store that vends
All kinds of bagels for your friends
Has generations serving you.
Order online or stand in queue.

18

After mornings when they are taught,
This playground is a sunny spot
For students who excel in school.
Getting ahead is how they rule.

19

If you miss this, it's not your fault.
The entrance is a banker's vault.
It speaks to felons who "banked" here.
They are all gone, so do not fear.

20

Two sisters bought this land, on which
A playhouse sprung that had a niche.
This is a gem of restoring,
Presenting work that's not boring.

21

Where people once were housed to serve,
One stands to hear a diverse verve
Of indie bands and local acts.
Head on down for the latest tracks.

22

That's right! It's sawdust on the floor.
It's Olde New York inside the door.
Roosevelt, Grant, and Lincoln drank.
Houdini left behind a prank.

23

No matter what the temp outdoors,
One sheds one's clothes to open pores.
It's cold. It's warm. It's wet and dry.
To come here, you should not be shy.

Greenwich Village & West Village

These two neighborhoods are famously known for their bohemian counterculture and as the home of New York University. These scavenger hunt clues can be found south of 14th Street, east of Hudson Street and Eighth Avenue, north of Houston Street, and west of the Bowery and Fourth Avenue.

1

If the postman would come to call,
They'd have to be extremely tall.
To orient where this is hung,
You look around for people young.

2

A ticket splashed across the bricks
Reads "gates" will open up at six
To legendary music club,
Where punk and new wave were a hub.

3

The rangers roam across the street
From where gay crowds were known to meet.
The space commemorates the rights
Of people who marched several nights.

4

The building's name was handed down
From a faraway seaside town.
The dramatists still take the stage
To hope their musings will engage.

5

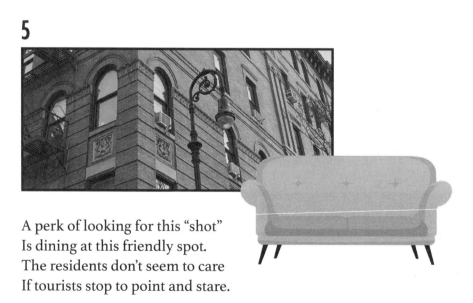

A perk of looking for this "shot"
Is dining at this friendly spot.
The residents don't seem to care
If tourists stop to point and stare.

6

His arms are flung so open-wide,
As if he were a tourist guide.
Our history recalls this "champ"
Who even has a postage stamp.

7

The elevated IRT
Was heard above the courtroom plea.
This gem escaped the wrecking ball,
When local friends faced city hall.

8

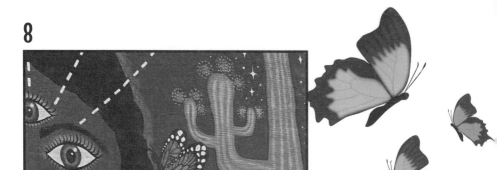

The largest mural in this town
Is where one gets a cap and gown:
High in the sky and undersea,
An ode to creativity.

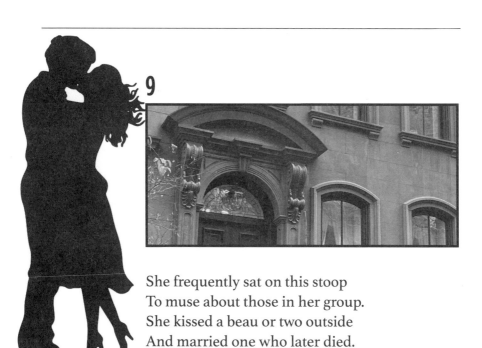

9

She frequently sat on this stoop
To muse about those in her group.
She kissed a beau or two outside
And married one who later died.

10

They make you laugh. They make you cry.
At times, you're not even sure why.
The Village has a bunch of clubs.
This isn't one that's for the schlubs.

11

He's looking up Fifth Avenue,
A street he never could review.
He's noted for his bravery
Both here and east, across the sea.

12

Despite its width at nine feet plus,
This house has often caused a fuss
When nearby actors saying lines
Sparked writers known to make headlines.

_____

_____

13

This crossroads of a history
Inspires the structure one will see.
It honors those whose lives were lost:
An epidemic's dreadful cost.

_____

_____

14

Farm cows and pigs were once outside,
When uptown wasn't dignified.
Though it looks like a Village place,
It moved four miles to find this space.

15

A statue with a sense of flair
Is standing in this tiny "square."
Cartographers might disagree.
There is no square, as one will see.

16

These row homes back into a court.
From window boxes, flowers sport.
The private homes inside the gate
Are priced beyond their modest state.

17

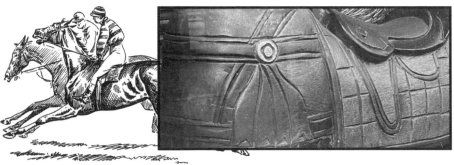

What's nearby is the riverbank,
Where after work they often drank.
Here still it serves up stew and brew.
They come to watch the races, too.

18

Some think this park misses the mark.
Yet concrete towns are dull and dark
'Til a small space that's underfed
Flourishes as a flowerbed.

19

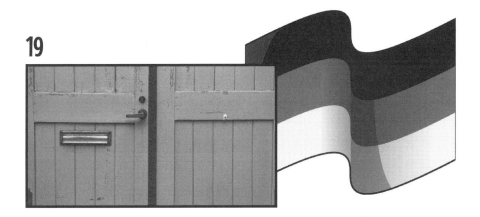

Coaches once were brought here to stay
Until the light of one more day.
Behind this door, now people seek
To brush up on German technique.

20

This building once held many stalls
To give support to frantic calls
From people who required a douse
Of water that would save their house.

_____

_____

21

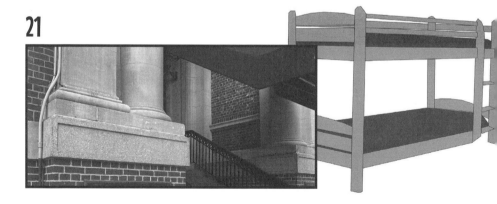

A home away for those who sail,
Right near the ships that they would hail.
It's still a place where travelers head
To bunk alone or in bunk beds.

_____

_____

22

Though designed for the middle class,
This "flathouse" has a lot of sass.
It's west of Seventh Avenue
Along a street which is askew.

23

Its German style may seem severe,
A center that we hold so dear.
From book to stage, it's journeyed far.
Their unknown troupes may yield a star.

Midtown East

A busy mix of residential living and businesses is featured in the scavenger hunt of Midtown East between 14th and 59th streets, east of Fifth Avenue (not including businesses on Fifth Avenue), and west of the East River.

1

The inspiration for this bronze
Is where they started marathons.
It turns its back on Edward Koch
To keep the prey on closest watch.

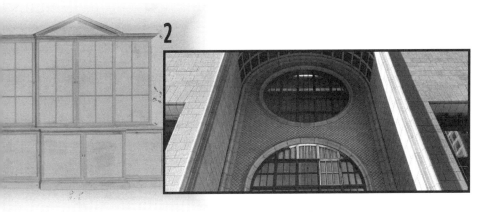

It's been HQ for big tech brands,
But ownership has since changed hands.
A "modern" firm designed this space,
And now their style is commonplace.

3

At first, you'd think this house is bland
Amidst a block that's midtown grand.
An architect, a famous name,
Together brought this place its fame.

4

From here Ol' Blues Eyes rarely strayed.
A former prez, he moved and stayed.
The suites are named for royalty,
The name derives from Germany.

_____

_____

5

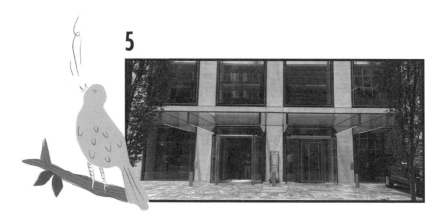

When it was built to habitate,
No reason to exaggerate,
It was the highest place to buy,
Four blocks from where the songbirds fly.

_____

_____

6

Compared to others, it is small,
But how about that waterfall?
In winter months, when there's a storm,
They heat the vents to keep it warm.

7

If you're a mad man in a crunch,
Stop by in summer for the lunch.
Or, if you seek community,
This is your opportunity.

8

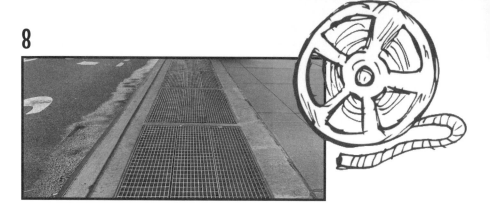

This grate is great for subway air,
So Hollywood filmed something there.
The scene "stands" out from all the rest.
It's iconic for how she dressed.

_____

_____

9

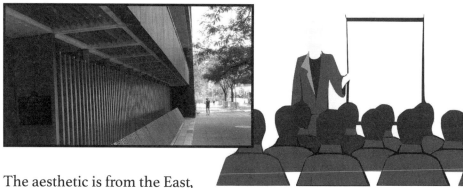

The aesthetic is from the East,
A sleek and subtle, visual feast.
The prince arrived to dedicate
A time when we cooperate.

_____

_____

10

It's private here behind the gate,
Where once you'd find a stablemate.
They're modified for homes and work.
Historians have saved this "quirk."

11

Take taxis down Park Avenue,
With any luck, you'll drive right through.
Below the street, the trains go by,
The clock outside will catch your eye.

12

From Broadway plays to Hollywood,
Her spirit shone for womanhood.
When in New York, she was at ease,
For Turtle Bay, she fought for trees.

_____

_____

13

This masterpiece of '30s style
Has eagle heads that never smile,
Plus radiator caps with wings,
Among so many other things.

_____

_____

14

This little guy says come inside
To see our friends that often guide.
You learn about the derring-do
Or find the one that looks like you.

15

When people speak of crowded space,
Like we are rats stuck in a race,
Three words are all you need to say
When you invoke this getaway.

16

A place you find our Uncle Sam
Is fortified like Hoover Dam.
Across the way, the land is wide,
Because you're at the riverside.

17

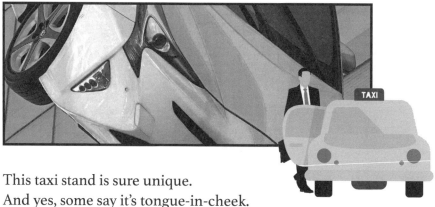

This taxi stand is sure unique.
And yes, some say it's tongue-in-cheek.
For those who show up at this spot,
Some cry when they receive a shot.

18

Below the street, the number six
Is where New Yorkers intermix.
The door is closed, so it seems odd
To see this sign on the façade.

19

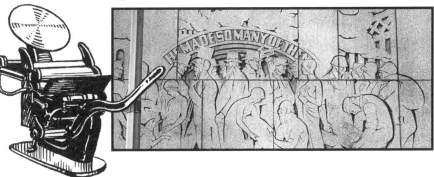

The common man is prominent
Where printed news was dominant.
The printing press has gone awry,
But TV crews and jazz stand by.

20

The neighborhood does radiate
From the park that's behind the gate.
The residents do hold the keys
To sit inside, among the trees.

21

With alcohol prohibited,
The barkeep here revisited.
A florist's name adored the sign,
But still they served liquor and wine.

22

In fall each year, the city stops.
The roads are closed and full of cops.
Assemble here is what they do
From far away, like Timbuktu.

23

From Gutenberg to Poe and Twain
And manuscripts by Charlemagne,
The founder brought them to this manse
But made his fortune in finance.

Midtown

When visitors think of New York City, they most likely think of Midtown, where Broadway shines, historic skyscrapers loom, and the largest and most luxurious stores in the country are located. There's so much to see, we've added four clues to this scavenger hunt. Find them between 14th and 59th streets, on Fifth Avenue, and west of Fifth Avenue to Eighth Avenue.

1

It's not a street; it's not a road.
No cars allowed or they'll be towed.
It's halfway past Sixth Avenue.
Pedestrians will all pass through.

2

They went the way of many stores:
The rent went up, they closed the doors.
A new crew said, "I want my shot."
Here's hoping they've a winning plot.

_____

_____

3

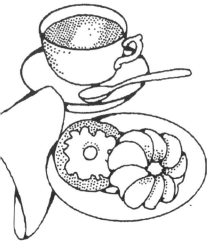

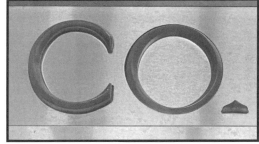

To eat a breakfast here's divine.
There's never much of any line.
So grab a Danish, glance inside,
And dream of life that's starry-eyed.

_____

_____

His plays achieved enormous fame.
For him, this building bears his name.
He wrote not of how faithful sing,
But they've camped here for worshipping.

_____

_____

5

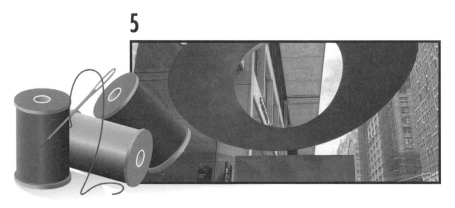

To learn to sew just like a pro,
One takes a class that's not much dough,
But most who journey to these blocks
Study design of couture frocks.

_____

_____

6

Peruse this book, a clue southbound.
That's where this predecessor's found,
The worshippers of any kind
Will come inside for peace of mind.

7

The first of these was near the site
Where flowers bloom and birds take flight.
This is the fourth to bear the name
Where many come to watch a game.

8

For holidays, the crowds will stop
Outside to stare, while others shop.
The prices here on Fifth are high,
So be prepared to bat an eye.

9

Slabs of concrete are its façade.
Its architecture is quite "mod."
Before it took up crafty trade,
City tourists came here for aid.

10

There's so much at this grand complex.
People don't know where to look next.
This mosaic depicts the thought
That evil's work will come to naught.

_____

_____

11

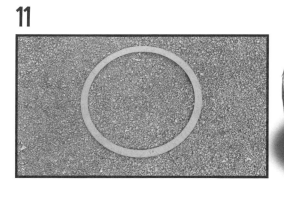

If "bocce ball" is what you say
When watching those intent at play,
They'll turn and glance and say, "Mon dieu,
You know not of this game's milieu."

_____

_____

12

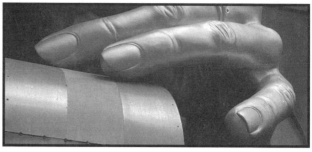

Where once the madams strolled the street,
The tourists know where they can meet
The movie stars and heads of state
Who silently stand still and wait.

13

On Sunday nights straight up at eight,
The TV crowd was never late
To see the stars of Liverpool,
Though no one thought the host was cool.

14

A temple for some troupes that dance,
Where Broadway gets a second chance.
A Moorish theme defines this site,
Where Shriners once enjoyed the night.

_____

_____

15

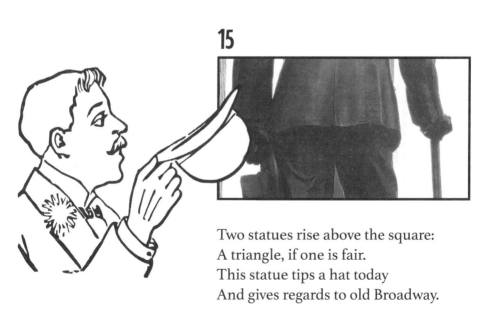

Two statues rise above the square:
A triangle, if one is fair.
This statue tips a hat today
And gives regards to old Broadway.

_____

_____

16

Fragrances here cannot be beat
Outside in cold or with June heat.
A palm tree for your inner court,
Or find a rose for your consort.

17

His name is blazoned in the lights
Where actors take the stage at nights.
Though many know his famous voice,
It's theater that was his choice.

18

There is more news than fit to print.
Their advertisers took the hint.
So digital is where one goes
To find the crooks that they expose.

19

In almost every town there's one,
This one's so huge, a visit's fun.
The smell alone of the perfume
Enchant us so that we'll consume.

20

As cities go, this isn't one.
A concert here won't be outdone.
It's part of one's vernacular
That here you find spectaculars.

21

From 53rd to Tokyo,
This trendy store is apropos
Of art one sees across the street,
Where cultures clash and moderns meet.

22

The guy who lent his famous name
Built libraries, to much acclaim.
You practice hard to make "the bill"
To show the world a special skill.

23

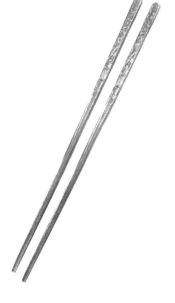

To bank or shop or see a chum,
But food is why most people come.
At noon or five or late at night,
The barbecue is out of sight.

24

No one admires its present space.
Its predecessor had such grace.
So there are plans to renovate,
Though endlessly, the pols debate.

25

A bookish girl once lived below
The roof that's like a French chateau.
Come by and sip a cup of tea,
An afternoon of pleasantry.

26

There's hardly one who's never heard
About this place near 33rd.
By day its base is rather plain,
At night, its crown will entertain.

27

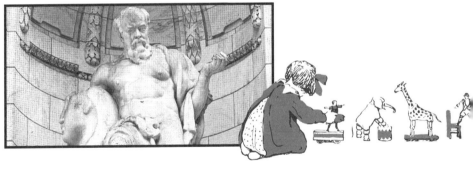

Outside there are two carnivores,
So walk quickly to the front door.
The main room features skies of blue.
Downstairs are toys, plus Tigger, too.

Midtown West

Well-known neighborhoods such as Chelsea and Hell's Kitchen are part of Midtown West along with Hudson Yards, the newest residential, retail, and entertainment complex in the city. Broadway patrons dine on Eighth and Ninth avenues and people shop for cars along 11th Avenue. This scavenger hunt stretches from 14th to 59th Street and Eighth Avenue to the Hudson River.

1

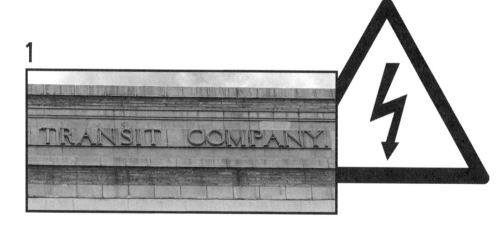

From 96 to Battery,
This place cooks up the energy
That once gave rise to subway cars,
Where people held to handlebars.

2

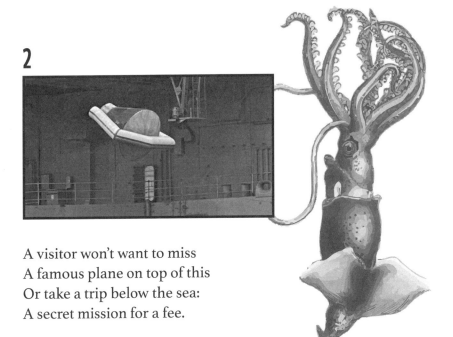

A visitor won't want to miss
A famous plane on top of this
Or take a trip below the sea:
A secret mission for a fee.

3

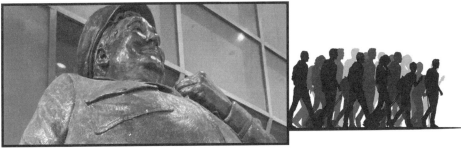

It's busier than any place.
The traffic's at a crazy pace.
Outside, a statue made of bronze:
One of TV's famous icons.

4

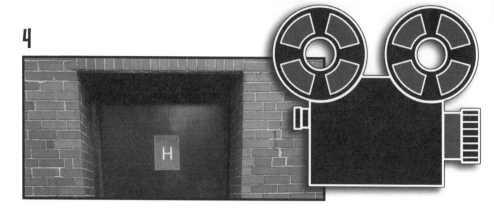

Sometimes celebrities are seen
Riding inside a limousine.
They tape an entertainment quip
That may become a news site clip.

5

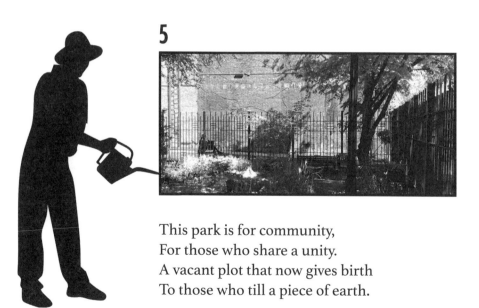

This park is for community,
For those who share a unity.
A vacant plot that now gives birth
To those who till a piece of earth.

6

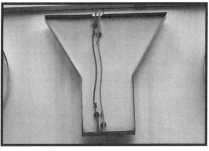

The who's-who of the dance elite
Will take the stage on their fleet feet.
Their season takes most of the year;
Still, other companies appear.

7

Even in New York it reigns large,
Especially 'cause there's no charge.
Its oddly shaped material
Hearkens to the ethereal.

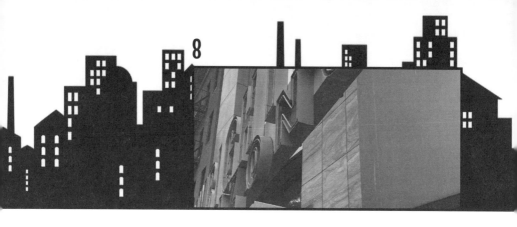

8

Before it was re-energized,
This "row" of town was publicized
Not as a place to take in art,
But find someone they called a "tart."

9

One doesn't even have to ask
If here one finds the food of Basque.
'Cause all the tastes of this nation
Are offered for the gustation.

10

To some it is a daily grind,
Yet people line up here to find
A comic take on news headlines.
It just shows how it takes all kinds.

11

The occupants that live inside
Are often taken for a ride.
As evening comes to Central Park,
The guides come here to disembark.

12

The Lusitania stopped by,
When cruising was so dignified.
Now it's become a sporting hall:
To swim, to skate, or hit a ball.

13

With cuisine from around the world
This single block has banners furled.
Reserve a meal or stop to graze
Before and after Broadway plays.

14

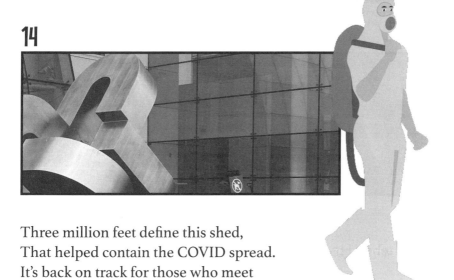

Three million feet define this shed,
That helped contain the COVID spread.
It's back on track for those who meet
To see the newest of the fleet.

15

No explanation's on the wall
About these creatures, strange and small.
Beside this globe, a spinning wheel
Makes one wonder, "What is the deal?"

16

From those who own the Circle Line,
This cruise features seafood divine.
A season pass keeps one afloat,
Eat here or on their sister boat.

17

If money is the main excuse
For not going to Syracuse,
Consider this a substitute
For traveling a direct route.

18

An alphabet of stores beyond
Is one reason people are fond
Of shopping for a gourmet treat
As tourists and the locals meet.

19

Where once the altar "boyz" sang prayers
At the bottom of many stairs,
Actors partake in daily wage
When they act up or play downstage.

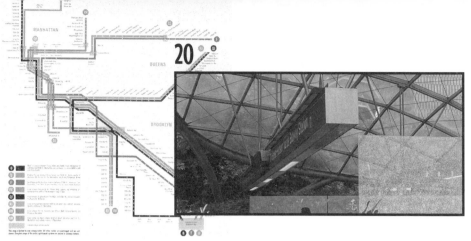

20

Count nearly 500 of these,
But give or take this number, please.
This line stretches out to the west.
Its entrance is one of the best.

21

A mile and a half names its length.
The distance is but just one strength.
To walk above the city streets
Is one of many wondrous treats.

22

When sending posts to NYC,
They first came to this property.
Now redone for another sort,
A grand new hall to help transport.

23

A telescoping outer shell
Makes way for space where artists dwell.
Thousands can now enjoy the night
Or daytime work that's dynamite.

Upper East Side

Considered by many as the most exclusive residential address in Manhattan, the Upper East Side is also known for its outstanding museums. The clues in this scavenger hunt section are located between 59th and 96th streets and east of Fifth Avenue (not including Central Park), and west of the East River.

1

From near and far, the subjects range
To help promote a free exchange.
There are films, talks, and poetry
For those in this society.

2

A simple lunch with malted shake
Or cherry pie and piece of cake.
Ignore the name above the store.
You'll find inside there's so much more.

_____

_____

3

This statue once swam with the fish,
But dreams come true, when there's a wish.
The cops found it below the waves
And brought it home to cheers and raves.

_____

_____

4

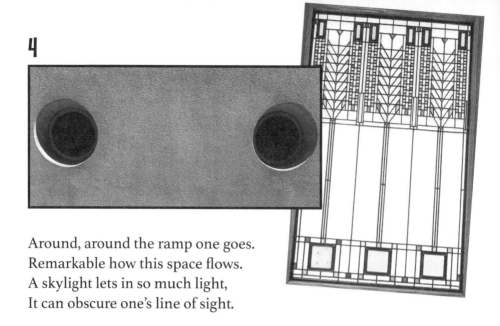

Around, around the ramp one goes.
Remarkable how this space flows.
A skylight lets in so much light,
It can obscure one's line of sight.

5

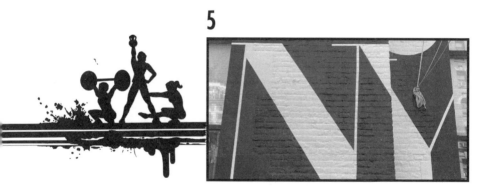

When COVID came they went online
To find an audience divine.
They rebranded a well-known name,
So people would embrace their aim.

6

Inside these doors, exhibits shine,
Sometimes of art, which was a "sign."
They illustrate some graphic work
At which some folks will laugh or smirk.

_____

_____

7

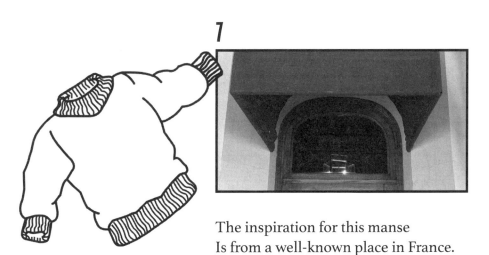

The inspiration for this manse
Is from a well-known place in France.
Today, among those on this strand,
Are shoppers of a famous brand.

_____

_____

8

Be careful. If you raise your hand,
You might have won a prize unplanned.
A Warhol or a Nike sneak
Can be offered in any week.

_____

_____

9

There's nothing like it on this coast.
Portland has one that it can boast.
When it flies off to island land,
Behold! It's Queens: a wonderland.

*Courtesy Chris Light
via Wikimedia Commons*

_____

_____

10

Along a numbered avenue,
A single pole may seem askew.
Atop it is a watch that stops,
No relevance to nearby shops.

11

A Brooklyn guy calls this his flat,
Though some call him a bureaucrat.
Where once it was a country home,
Now city dwellers often roam.

12

One goes back to a simpler time,
When penny candy wasn't a dime.
All the sweets that come to mind
Are why this store is well-designed.

13

The dames in charge of this hotel
Have turned it into something swell.
It hearkens back to genteel ways,
When visitors arrived for days.

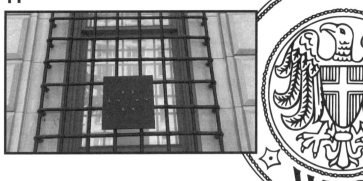

Inside these rooms, Vienna waits,
An era's art to celebrate.
A hundred years or more passed by,
And yet it's modern to the eye.

15

The Guinness Book records the crime
Of thievery that was big-time.
They heisted jewels and got away
Precisely after New Year's Day.

16

 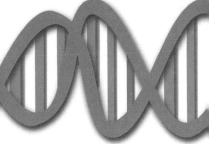

Along the river, through these gates,
Beneath this dome, a world awaits.
Events and lectures fill your head,
Especially of bio-med.

_____

_____

17

A comrade of one Henry Frick
Once lived inside this home of brick.
The steel supports came from his mill,
And now his name is joined with "hill."

_____

_____

18

For 80 years, the meat's been made:
A butcher shop above the grade.
One stops inside or snacks outside,
And orders can be shipped worldwide.

19

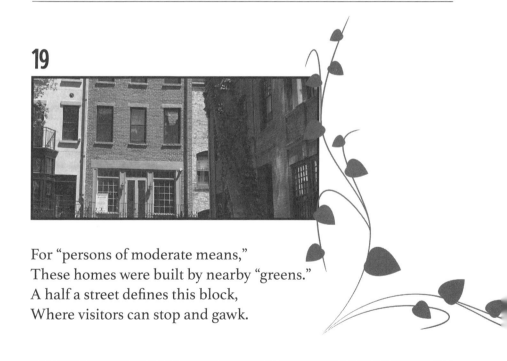

For "persons of moderate means,"
These homes were built by nearby "greens."
A half a street defines this block,
Where visitors can stop and gawk.

20

Before this man bought any art,
His story had a humble start.
Creating coke to help make steel
Became his most resourceful deal.

21

This esplanade is nine miles long
And often brings a healthy throng.
The sign reflects a person's stride
Across this island far and wide.

22

They started with a faddish skirt.
Then came uptown to reassert
Their visionary shopping sense
To offer wares not spare, but dense.

23

Militiamen once graced this hall,
And tennis players came to call.
Now the arts are camped inside.
To have a show here's dignified.

Central Park

The most famous urban park in America has so many wondrous places to explore that we've added extra clues in this scavenger hunt section. Central Park is located between 59th and 110th streets, Fifth Avenue, and Central Park West.

1

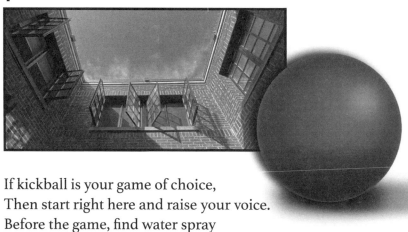

If kickball is your game of choice,
Then start right here and raise your voice.
Before the game, find water spray
And rocks to climb and swings for play.

2

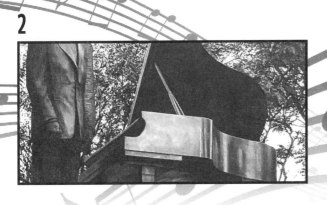

His piano is high and dry.
If he's inspired, his hands might fly
And give the world another chance
To acclaim his musical stance.

3

It was a stop to give some shade
For those part of the carriage trade.
Off the road with rocks that can wow,
It's perfect for a wedding vow.

4

Before Olmsted designed the park,
Militia here would disembark.
The city took over command
To help design this wonderland.

5

This is the fourth one to go 'round,
And when it whirls, you hear the sound
With chariots that kids adore.
But after dark, they close the door.

6

They thought the British might come forth.
They built this to defend the north.
Around the rise, the park did grow.
Ascend on high to see the show.

7

This stone was found in feet of sand,
And when they wanted it to stand,
The crabs were added for support.
See them nearby the Delacorte.

8

The gardens three are all well-known,
Inviting one to walk alone.
From a birdbath that's held on high,
There's a secret garden to spy.

_____

_____

9

The winds will blow and blow all day,
And on some nights come out to play.
They line each morn and hope for shade,
To see stuff of which dreams are made.

_____

_____

10

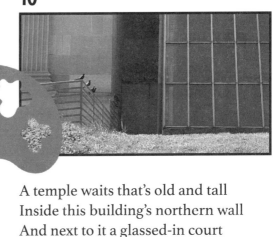

A temple waits that's old and tall
Inside this building's northern wall
And next to it a glassed-in court
With sculptures of a newer sort.

11

In early morn and nearing dark,
See dogs off-leash who romp and bark.
This native dog ignores that ban.
He strides along a hunting man.

12

A hero who was all the rage
Was honored in the Gilded Age.
Beside him stood this Nike sprite.
They're facing south to show their might.

_____

_____

13

The waterfalls are all man-made,
A cooling mist under the shade.
To find this place, start at East Drive
Near a rink where skaters do strive.

_____

_____

14

Twenty-five are set up for play.
The young and old, they come each day.
One turns their back on views of green
To wage battles and claim the queen.

15

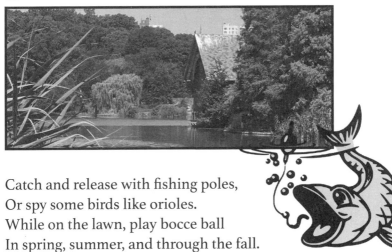

Catch and release with fishing poles,
Or spy some birds like orioles.
While on the lawn, play bocce ball
In spring, summer, and through the fall.

16

The steps were made for kids to climb
While they recite a tale of rhyme,
Or just because they like the girl
Who's caught up in a party whirl.

17

The songs are heard at every hour
With quiet voice or sung with power.
A mosaic of just one word,
The dreams of many here are heard.

18

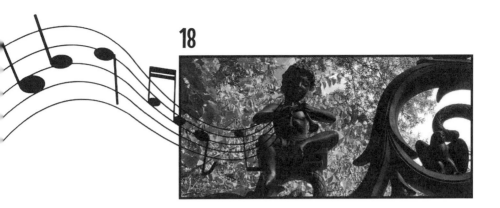

A dancing boy with singing birds,
This piper plays above the herds.
When passing through this iron gate,
If after five, it is too late.

19

From *Gilded Age* to *Home Alone*,
This famous place is often shown.
When stepping back from fountain spray,
One sees the walls where murals stay.

20

Here dolls on string will give a show,
Not Broadway-esque, but apropos
For kids who like their bedtime tales
With lessons learned, where good prevails.

21

At one time milk was hard to find,
So park officials were inclined
To offer it and snacks for those
Who played nearby in the meadows.

22

In Queens it was a World's Fair thrill.
It's now atop the Cedar Hill.
This statue shows a man who sought
To unite lands that often fought.

23

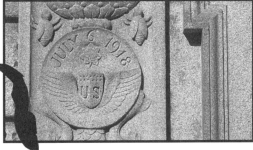

The runners race around the track.
Below, one stops to read a plaque
To learn about a leading foe,
A reformer of status quo.

24

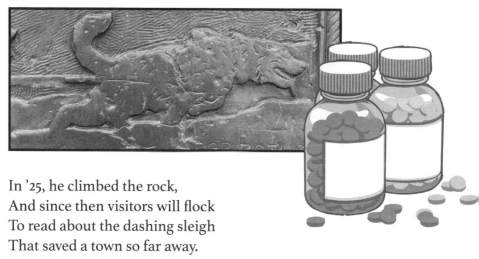

In '25, he climbed the rock,
And since then visitors will flock
To read about the dashing sleigh
That saved a town so far away.

_____

_____

25

The name describes what one can view
Of fields where there is derring-do,
A pond that once was named a lake,
A place where lonely hearts will ache.

_____

_____

Upper West Side & Morningside Heights

This scavenger hunt section includes the largely residential area of the Upper West Side, Riverside Park, and Morningside Heights, known for its colleges and medical institutions. Search for clues north of 59th Street, east of the Hudson River, south of 125th Street/Martin Luther King Boulevard, and west of Morningside Avenue/Manhattan Avenue and Central Park West.

1

Embedded in the promenade
Are names of those who made the grade.
One looks and looks, but finds no road,
'Cause here the ships would bring their load.

2

Three hundred thousand come each year,
Which tells you why it is so dear.
If it should rain, one's kids can play
Inside this space most every day.

3

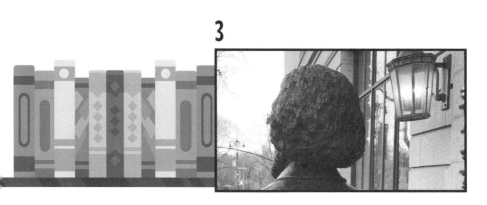

He gained his freedom in the North,
And on the north, he does hold forth.
With lectures and a special tour,
This place explains the man's allure.

4

The coffee comes with whipping cream.
The refills are a student's dream.
In Budapest, they're everywhere.
In Morningside, pull up a chair.

5

Three architects converge nearby.
Bold new towers reach toward the sky.
To find the waterfall that's spry,
One stands below the road up high.

6

Their mission is empowerment.
It has been quite an instrument
To give women a place to shine
And hear a voice that's genuine.

_____

_____

7

The bear looks down over the rock
To see a faun who's not in shock.
Presumably, it plays a song;
In this fountain, they get along.

_____

_____

8

Around this famed memorial
Are tributes to a man whose role
To protect land in Yellowstone
May not always be that well-known.

9

Since '34, this place to stop
Has coffee ground inside the shop.
The deli's fame is nationwide,
Beyond Manhattan's western side.

From foreign land, a gift was sent.
But on the way an accident,
Which meant the ceremony slipped
Until the trees could be reshipped.

11

Exclusion was a driving force
To give many another course
To achieve learned prominence
And fight the white-male dominance.

12

Just to the south, the voices soar.
Then, to the west, is Broadway's door.
This art suggests a simple chit.
To get inside, one will need it.

13

Beside a church that's grand in scale,
A statue tells a grander tale,
Where good defeats an evil force,
So peace can glimmer in due course.

14

A statue faced a park of green,
But some thought it should not be seen.
Out to the West, the statue shipped.
His legacy lives on in "script."

_____

_____

15

A few steps from a nearby park,
An artist's work has made a mark.
A museum of one man's work.
It's free to view, a special perk.

_____

_____

16

It's residential homes today,
But once musicians came to play.
Billie Holiday sang right here,
But only for an engineer.

_____

_____

17

A school once took this vacant plot
And gave it life, with plants and thought.
A park where chickens come to roost,
It gives the neighborhood a boost.

_____

_____

18

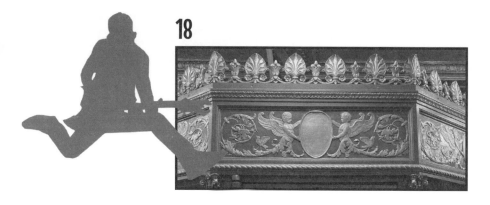

The talkies once were on the screen,
But now it hosts a different scene.
Comedians and rockers rule.
A movie palace that turned cool.

_____

_____

19

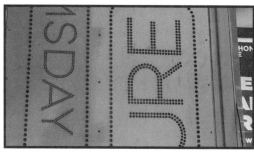

They shot a scene from _Annie Hall_,
It is a moment to recall.
This place has never lost its fame,
Attracting crowds to much acclaim.

_____

_____

20

Each fall, they come to congregate,
To reaffirm and dedicate
Heroic acts these servants make.
Each day they put their lives at stake.

21

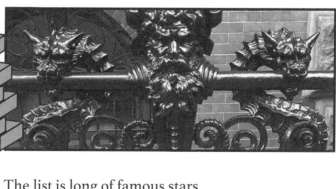

The list is long of famous stars
Who lived beyond these iron bars.
Its name is something of a guess.
They may have borrowed from the West.

The figure holds aloft a sword,
But not to fight against the horde.
It prays for guidance from on high,
A youthful gaze up to the sky.

23

At her feet, it is always green,
A simple but affecting scene.
In early life, New York was home.
Throughout the world, her deeds are known.

East Harlem

East Harlem was a historically Italian neighborhood that is now known as Spanish Harlem or *El Barrio*. Search for clues north of 96th Street, east of Fifth Avenue, and south and west of the East River.

Adjacent to the Metro train
Is where a street art has domain.
Each year they start again with white
To spray an art that's out of sight.

2

In *U.S. News* and *World Report,*
They recognize these kids' transport
To achievement in other schools
When they prepare and have the tools.

3

Come have a cup of great coffee
With palm trees found on the marquee.
For breakfast, lunch, and dinner, too,
Like heading south with this menu.

4

When architects planned this *masjid*,
They purposely built it off-grid.
Its striking dome and minaret
Create a site you won't forget.

_____

_____

5

"I wonder as I wander here,"
Is there a ghost who's writing near?
Ask him for his learned response
About the Harlem Renaissance.

_____

_____

6

This artwork might just "grow" on you,
Depending on your point of view.
It's in the center of a space
Beside a special senior place.

7

When this was just a village green,
Horses would stable in between
The houses to its west and east.
Since then, the prices have increased.

8

Connecting those from distant shores
Is one reason to come indoors.
Good hospitality's observed
With diverse foods, as guests are served.

9

A pope donated a gemstone
For this statue that is well-known.
In many languages they praise
And celebrate on festive days.

10

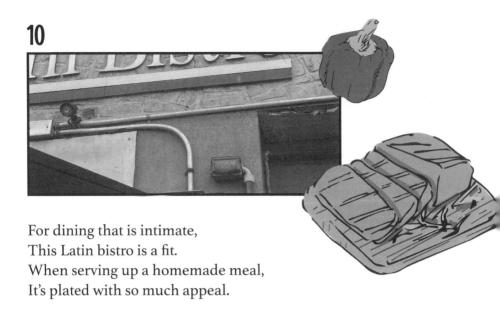

For dining that is intimate,
This Latin bistro is a fit.
When serving up a homemade meal,
It's plated with so much appeal.

11

Tomorrow's wind might bring a squall,
But this sculpture will never fall.
Majestically it does rise
To reflect rays of sunny skies.

12

Celebrities are known to dine
And brag that they can "skip the line."
A "Southern" fare for family,
The heart and soul of Italy.

13

It found a place right on the "mile"
To showcase culture of an isle.
The visitors can now immerse
Themselves with Latin art and verse.

14

It's comic that it bears the name
Of guys who filmed a football game
But joked that anyone could play
And take the ball to win the day.

_____

_____

15

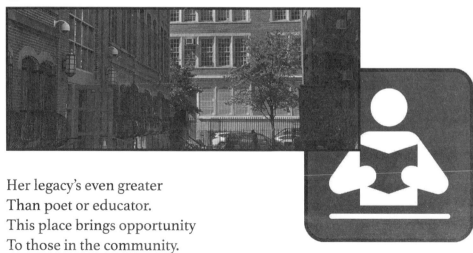

Her legacy's even greater
Than poet or educator.
This place brings opportunity
To those in the community.

_____

_____

16

From vintage clocks to balconies
Or Beaux Arts ornamental frieze,
The owners seek to search and find
Neglected pieces left behind.

17

One can get kicks most anywhere,
But at this branch, look in the air
To see styles of sneaker folklore
Before one walks inside the door.

18

All things New York are on the walls,
Like artifacts or dollhouse dolls.
It celebrates all five boroughs,
From Forest Hills to Fresh Meadows.

19

El Barrio food with a flair:
They even offer vegan fare.
Inside, the space looks rather smart,
Showing contemporary art.

20

Benjamin Franklin would be proud
That this building attracts a crowd
Of students who are penny-wise.
To them, the learning is the prize.

21

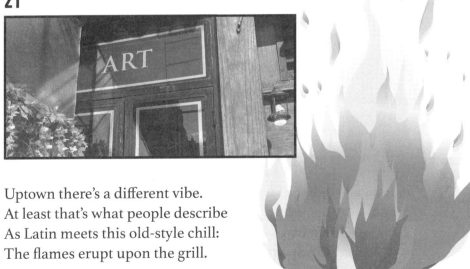

Uptown there's a different vibe.
At least that's what people describe
As Latin meets this old-style chill:
The flames erupt upon the grill.

22

For public health, they advocate
And offer books to educate.
One calls ahead for direction
For exploring the collection.

_____

_____

23

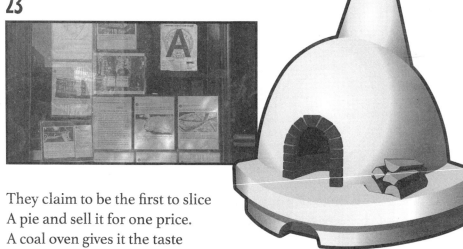

They claim to be the first to slice
A pie and sell it for one price.
A coal oven gives it the taste
Without using tomato paste.

_____

_____

Central Harlem & West Harlem

The sights, sounds, and smells of these two neighborhoods are what people outside of New York imagine when they the hear the word "Harlem." For purposes of this book, the scavenger hunt is defined as south of 155th Street, west of Fifth Avenue, north of Central Park North, and east of Morningside Avenue/Manhattan Avenue and the Hudson River.

1

From Africa and lands beyond,
Scholars are known to correspond.
All items shown are rarified
For anyone who comes inside.

2

Invisible, he'll never be.
By riverside now he can see
The park where he would often stride,
Across from where he lived and died.

3

This church began with 40 souls.
It grew, prospered, took on new roles,
And moved three blocks to spread the word,
To praise the Gospel so it's heard.

4

Handmade crafts and figurines
Are here, as well as denim jeans.
It's inside-out most every day.
Buy some pieces from far away.

_____

_____

5

How 'bout a classic with a twist
Or films atop your viewing list?
All summer long, this place will swing
Inside a park with everything.

_____

_____

6

A Sunni dome will catch your eye,
Reminding you of days gone by.
A minister spoke at this sight.
His words still ring out, strong and bright.

7

A must-stop on the foodie tour
For those in search of epicure,
This restaurant is known as "queen"
To Harlem folk who make the scene.

8

The "Hell Fighters" needed a spot
To drill, to meet, to get their "shot."
The city built this arsenal,
A structure that's remarkable.

9

A "sweet project" on country land,
This estate was considered grand.
In present times, the home was moved
Across the street to be improved.

A certain style of jazz was born
That's not likely to be timeworn.
Today they serve up jazz at night,
But come before and grab a bite.

11

Comfort

The premier place for comfort food:
The menu is bound to include
The Southern treats like chicken fried
Among the dishes served with pride.

12

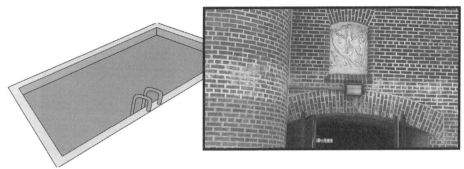

It takes its name from 42.
Around the bases the guy flew.
But here the sport is getting wet.
When it is hot, take off the sweat.

13

They come to skate in rain or snow.
They come for swimming, fast or slow.
And all the while, beneath the fun,
The water treatment work is done.

14

Promote, preserve, and present this.
They do more than just reminisce.
Unknown work that's bound to please
Comes from the stash of devotees.

15

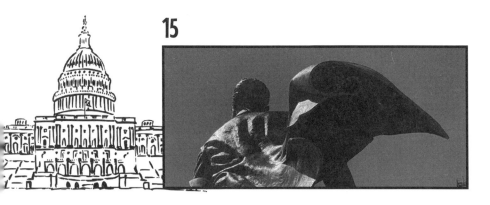

Even in bronze, the statue climbs,
A man who still transcends his times.
His work inside the Capitol,
Some thought he was a radical.

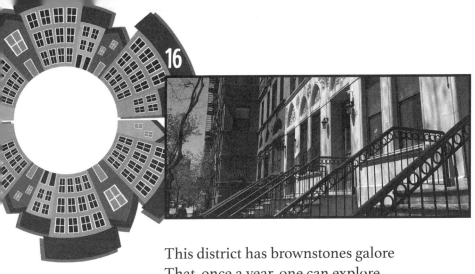

16

This district has brownstones galore
That, once a year, one can explore.
But one can see most every day
The Gilded Age is on display.

17

Courtesy Getty Images

Music, soul food, and artists meet
Where chefs inspire how people eat.
One sups at night or stops for lunch.
On Sundays there's a Gospel brunch.

18

Be sure to stop and look around
When taking trains that go uptown.
A colorful display awaits:
Mosaics of the Harlem greats.

19

There are 28 in a row.
All built in step so long ago.
Unusual for cityscapes
Are the different yards and shapes.

20

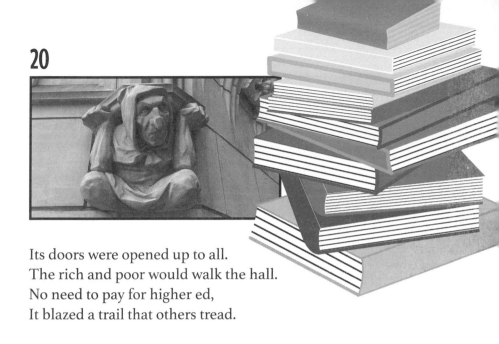

Its doors were opened up to all.
The rich and poor would walk the hall.
No need to pay for higher ed,
It blazed a trail that others tread.

21

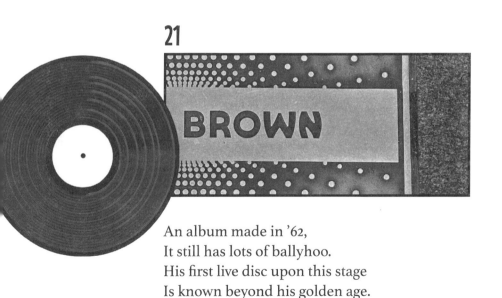

An album made in '62,
It still has lots of ballyhoo.
His first live disc upon this stage
Is known beyond his golden age.

22

This wicked park is small in size,
An oasis for friendly ties.
A greenish show gave it a boost.
A renovation it produced.

23

They focus on those three to eight
To help them to accentuate
Their curiosity to tell
The stories that they know so well.

Washington Heights & Inwood

At the northern tip of Manhattan, the generally flat landscape becomes hilly. When traveling through Washington Heights and Inwood, wear your hiking shoes. These two neighborhoods are north of 155th Street and surrounded by three bodies of water—the Hudson River, the Harlem River, and the East River.

1

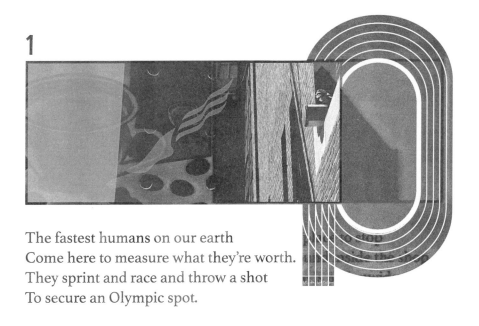

The fastest humans on our earth
Come here to measure what they're worth.
They sprint and race and throw a shot
To secure an Olympic spot.

2

When you order at this venue,
The famous food on the menu
Appears in more than 20 kinds,
Along with many drinks and wines.

_____

_____

3

This is a garden in a cove
That is a kind of treasure trove
For students from the nearby schools
Who learn to plant with garden tools.

_____

_____

4

Bird-watchers might come to the marsh,
Especially if the weather's harsh.
The egrets with a snowy sheen
Are often waiting to be seen.

5

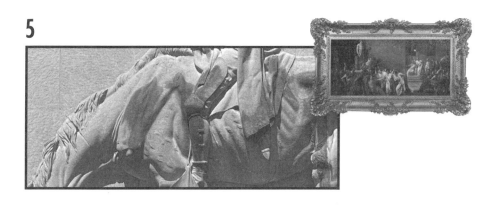

Come north to find El Dorado.
It closely ranks with the Prado.
The art of colonies inspired
A collection that is admired.

6

- *TILAPIA*
- *OREJITA*
- *MOLLEJITA*
- *PATICA DE CERDO*
- *POLLO GUISADO*

Dominican and Cuban fare
Yield sandwiches beyond compare.
Stop by for lunch or some rapport.
It's *abierto* 24.

7

Free exercise starts at this dock,
Where devotees will often flock.
Beginners can sign up to go
Out on the river for a row.

8

This building had a tenant whose
Career began with football news,
But concert halls were his calling.
Performances were enthralling.

9

If fusion fare is what you seek,
Then their approach may be unique:
Mixing up cuisine from the East
With Latin flavors for a feast.

10

If college sports give one a thrill,
Then just below an Inwood hill,
A stadium is primed for fall
When one can watch "ivy" football.

_____

_____

11

These little guys will come and go
While on their way to Mexico.
This tiny garden gives them space,
Where we can watch them fly with grace.

_____

_____

12

For many years, the maps portrayed
A promontory not man-made.
This burger joint recalls a time
When maritime was in the prime.

13

The oldest mansion on the isle,
Once housed a general in style.
It's called the "jewel in the crown"
In this section of NY town.

14

The Roxy Theatre compares
To this place with multiple stairs.
One climbs them to sit down to view
A movie or a music crew.

_____

_____

15

The Metropolitans were one
Of the sports teams that often won
At the site that is long since gone,
But still the legends linger on.

_____

_____

16

They claim to be *el rey* of this.
And in the window, one can't miss
That the entrée the owner likes
Is roasted on what looks like spikes.

17

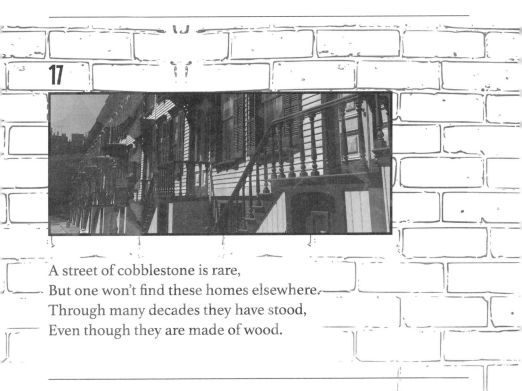

A street of cobblestone is rare,
But one won't find these homes elsewhere.
Through many decades they have stood,
Even though they are made of wood.

18

At one time farmers tilled this soil.
For generations they would toil
Until the city grew so near.
Now you can buy a souvenir.

19

The patrons profess loyalty
To chicharrón served every day.
This place claims to be royalty.
You'll find this one along Broadway.

20

When it is hot, this spot ranks high
For sipping drinks as boats rush by.
So watch the sun sink in the sky
As summer wanes and night is nigh.

21

A mountain biking course goes through
A park that features access to
Another borough where the Yanks
Are found to play near riverbanks.

22

A monastery of a sort
Is located within a "fort."
The largest room that's on display
Is typically where people pray.

_____

_____

23

The northern tip of Jersey's shore
Once shone this light to cry out for
The ships that lost their way at sea,
To bring them to their home safely.

_____

_____